To Jesus Christ, my Savior and King –
thank you for the humbling gifts of calling me Your
beloved daughter, blessing me with Your Church, and
allowing me to share a little of Your love
with the world.
-K.W.

For my Rosie,
that you will always delight in
the beauty of our faith.
-M.W.

Text copyright © 2020 Katie Warner
Illustrations copyright © 2020 Meg Whalen

All rights reserved. With the exception of short excerpts used in critical review, no part of this work may be reproduced, transmitted, or stored in any form whatsoever without prior written permission of the publisher.

Book design by Meg Whalen. The text for this book is set in Barteldes Small. The illustrations for this book were rendered in Procreate.

ISBN 978-1-5051-1793-6

Published in the United States by
TAN Books
PO Box 269
Gastonia, NC 28053
www.TANBooks.com

Printed in the United States of America

THIS IS THE CHURCH

written by Katie Warner
illustrated by Meg Whalen

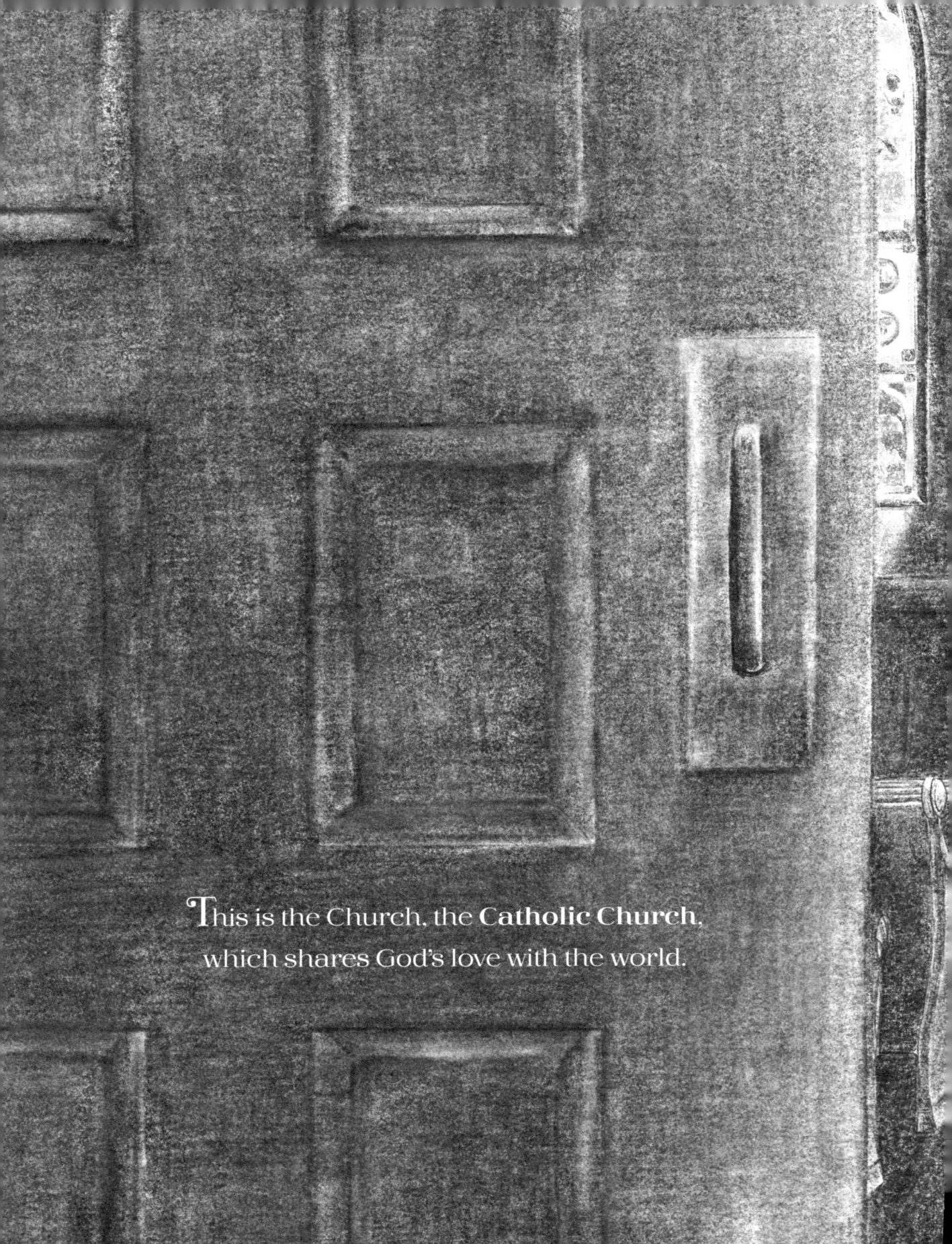

This is the Church, the **Catholic Church**, which shares God's love with the world.

This is **Christ Jesus**, our Savior and King,
who died and then rose and founded the Church,
the Catholic Church,
to share God's love with the world.

These are the apostles, filled with the Spirit.
They told of Christ Jesus, our Savior and King,
who died and then rose and founded the Church,
the Catholic Church,
to share God's love with the world.

These are Christ's parents,
Joseph and Mary.
To them was born Jesus,
our Savior and King,
who died and then rose
and founded the Church,
the Catholic Church,
to share God's love
with the world.

These are the Jews, God's chosen people.
For thousands of years they longed to be free.
God sent His Son, Jesus, our Savior and King,
who died and then rose
and founded the Church, the Catholic Church,
to share God's love with the world.

These are the patriarchs,
prophets, and kings,
who guided the Jews throughout history.
They awaited Christ Jesus,
our Savior and King,
who died and then rose
and founded the Church,
the Catholic Church,
to share God's love with the world.

ABRAHAM

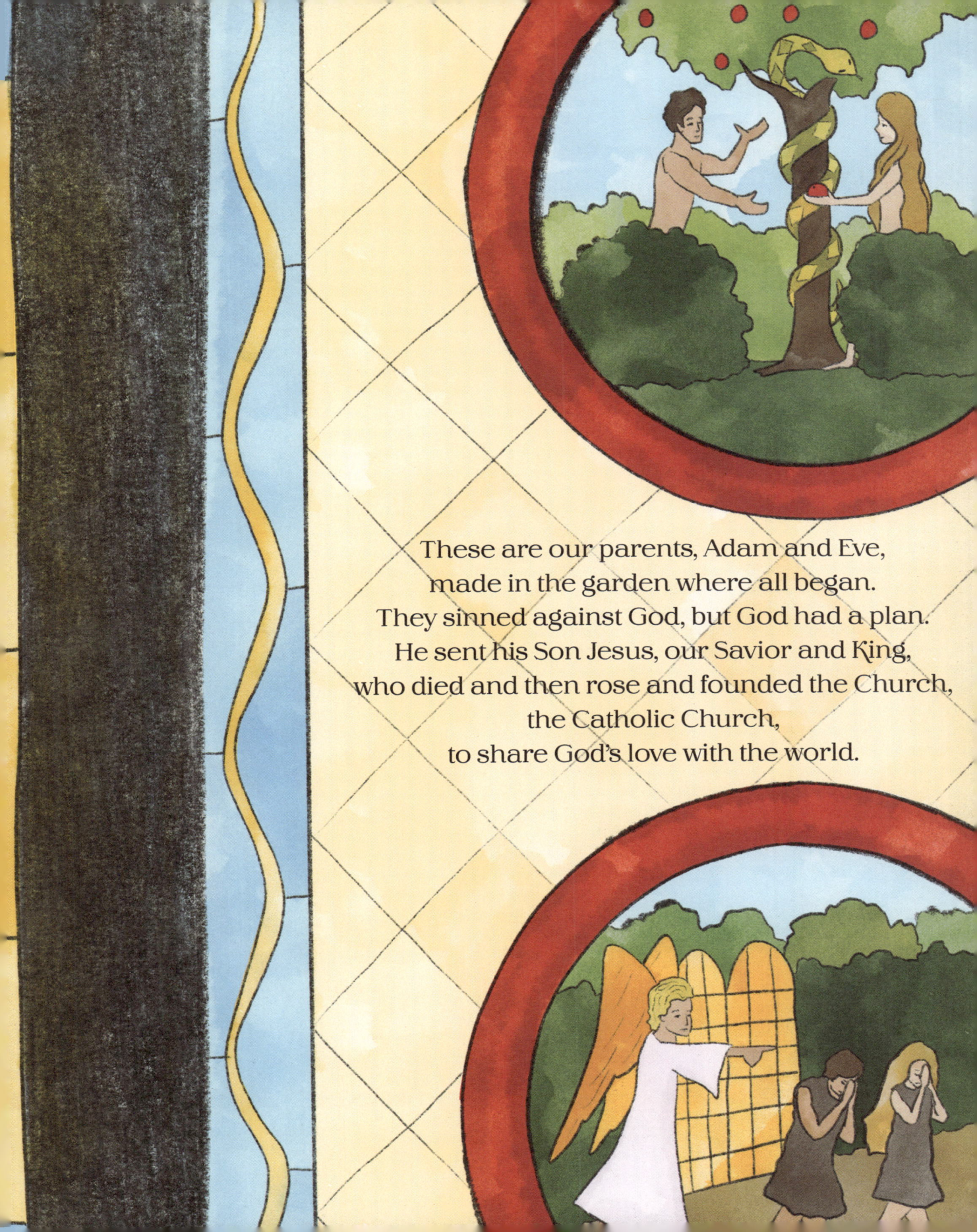

These are our parents, Adam and Eve,
made in the garden where all began.
They sinned against God, but God had a plan.
He sent his Son Jesus, our Savior and King,
who died and then rose and founded the Church,
the Catholic Church,
to share God's love with the world.

This is creation, wondrous and grand,
made by the power of God's mighty hand.
And the greatest creation of all was **man** —

Redeemed by Christ Jesus, our Savior and King,
who died and then rose and founded the Church,
the Catholic Church, to share God's love with the world.

This is you.

You are a part of God's great plan,
His plan for creation, wondrous and grand.
You show the power of God's mighty hand.

Your story begins with Adam and Eve,
who came before patriarchs, prophets, or kings,
before Christ's parents, Joseph and Mary,
and before the apostles, filled with the Spirit,
who spread the Good News we still share today:
God sent His Son, Jesus, our Savior and King,
who died and then rose and founded the Church,
the Catholic Church,
to share God's love with the world.

This is **your** Church,
the Catholic Church.

Go share God's love with the world.